Farmyard Friends

Editor: Eve Marleau
Designer: Melissa Alaverdy
Picture Researcher: Maria Joannou

Copyright © QEB Publishing, Inc. 2010

Published in the United States by
QEB Publishing, Inc.
3 Wrigley, Suite A
Irvine, CA 92618

www.qed-publishing.co.uk

A CIP record for this title is available from the Library of Congress.

ISBN 978 1 60992 060 9

Printed in China

Picture credits
(t=top, b=bottom, l=left, r=right, c=centre,
fc=front cover)
Alamy Images Blickwinkel/Hecker 12t, Andrew Fox 18 Picture Contact/
Ton Koene 19t, David R. Frazier Photolibrary, Inc. 24–25, Grant Heilman
Photography 26–27, Photogenix 57tl, Hazel Gwatkin 58t, Picture Partners
65t, Inga Spence 86tr; Corbis Louis
Laurent Grandadam 74-75, Justin Guariglia 76l, Wildlife GmbH 104tl;
Corbis Isabelle Vayron/Sygma 22, Alvis Upitis/AgStock Images 25tl, Ulrich
Baumgarten/Vario images 36l, Wayne Hutchinson 47t, Robert Polett/
AgStock Images 34-35, Michael St. Maur Sheil 53t, José Fuste Raga 54-55,
Anders Ryman 57tr, Vladimir Godnik/Moodboard 101t; **Getty Images**
Workbook Stock/John Zoiner 32-33, Dorling Kindersley/Simon Clay 37t,
Dorling Kindersley 38t, Dorling Kindersley/Geoff Dann 66l, Taxi/Marsi 99t,
Stone/Nicolas Russell 104-105; **Istockphoto** Morganl 25tr, The Image Bank/
Bob Elsdale 70, 71bl, Photographer's Choice/Georgette Douwma 71t, First
Light/Bert Klassen 72-73, Jean Michel Foujols 73t, AFP/Frederick Florin 78t,
Dorling Kindersley/Kim Taylor and Jane Burton 80t, Taxi/VCL 80b, Dorling
Kindersley/Peter Anderson 83t; **Photolibrary** Imagebroker.net/Hartmut
Schmidt 14, Philip Quirk 17tr, Imagebroker.net/Michael Krabs 18–19, Mark
Hamblin 20l, EA. Janes 20r, All Canada Photos/Ron Watts 20–21,
Robert Harding Travel/Mark Mawson 22–23, John Warburton-Lee Photography
27t;, Philippe Body 30l, Juniors Bildarchiv 30-31, 31t, 39t, 40t, 44-45, 46-47, Index
Stock Imagery/Grant Heilman Photography Inc 35t, Tips Italia/Bildagentur RM
36-37, Age Fotostock/EA. Janes 38-39, 40b, Imagebroker.net/Michael Krabs 41c,
Imagebroker.net/Helmut Meyer zur Capellen 42-43, Superstock/Clyde M Slade
43t, David Harrigan 51t, Sabine Lubenow 52-53, Nature Picture Library/Britain on
View 54, Agustin Catalan 56t, Cotswolds Photo Library 61t, Robin Smith 62-63,
Superstock 64l, Juniors Bildarchiv 66r;, Jeff Friedman 75t, Lasting Images 77b,
Alberto Paredes 78-79, Oxford Scientific Film/Roger de la Harpe 79t, Juniors
Bildarchiv 84-85b, Imagebroker.net/Alessandra Sarti 98t, Juniors Bildarchiv 98b,
Animals Animals/Phil Degginger 98-99, Jörgen Brennicke 100-101, Alain Christof
102l, Y Arthus-Bertrand 107tr; **Rex Features** East News 33t, Jussi Nukari 41t;
Shutterstock Eric Isselée 10l, MisterElements 11b, 13b, 15b, 171b, 13b, 15b, 17b,
25b, 226b, Aleks.K 10-11, Wikus Otto 11t, Sally Wallis 12–13, Jean Morrison 13t,
Nancy Gill 14–15, Laila Kazakevica 15t, Nando Viciano 16–17, Mikhail Malyshev
17tl, Jarno Gonzalez Zarraonandia 9t, Svry 23t, Volker Rauch 24, Pixel Memoirs
26t, (background), Thomas M Perkins 24b, MisterElements 31b, 33b, 36b, 37b,
51t, 43b, 45b, 46b, Dario Sabljak 34l, Jonson 45t, Graeme Dawes 46t, MisterElements 51b, 52b, 57b, 58br, 61b, 62b, 64r, 66r, Eric Isselée 50l, 67l, Cen 50-51, Oxana
Prokofyeva 52t, Walter Quirtmair 55t, Majeczka 56-57, Jean Frooms 58bl, Eric
Gevaert 59t, 59b, Rickshu 60-61, Robyn Mackenzie 62t, F franckreporter 64–65,
Eric Isselée 87t, Iakov Kalinin 80-81, MisterElements71br, 73b, 76r, 78b, 81bl, 83b,
84b, 86br, Hydromet 70-71, Arnaud Weisser 72l, Fat_fa_tin 72r, Ivaylo Ivanov 77t,
Tischenko Irina 81t, Lilya 81br, 86l, Smit 82-83, Thumb 84-85t, Monkey Business Im-
ages 85r, S.Cooper Digital 87b, MisterElements 91bl, 93b, 95b, 97bl, 99b, 100r, 103b,
104b, 107b, Postnikova Kristina 90-91, Zuzule 91t, 105tr, Karen Givens 91c, Nikitin
Anatoly Nikolaevich 91br, Dogist 92l, Vicki France 93-94, Scott Sanders 95l, Stanis-
lav Sokolov 94-95, Ivonne Wierink 95t, Stephanie Coffman 96-97, Marekuliasz 97t,
Elena Elisseeva 97br, Margo Harrison 100l, Karel Gallas 102r, D Kyslynskyy 103,
Craig McAteer 106-107.

Words in **bold** are explained in the Glossary on page 108.

Farmyard Friends

Camilla de la Bédoyère

QEB Publishing

Contents

Horses and Ponies

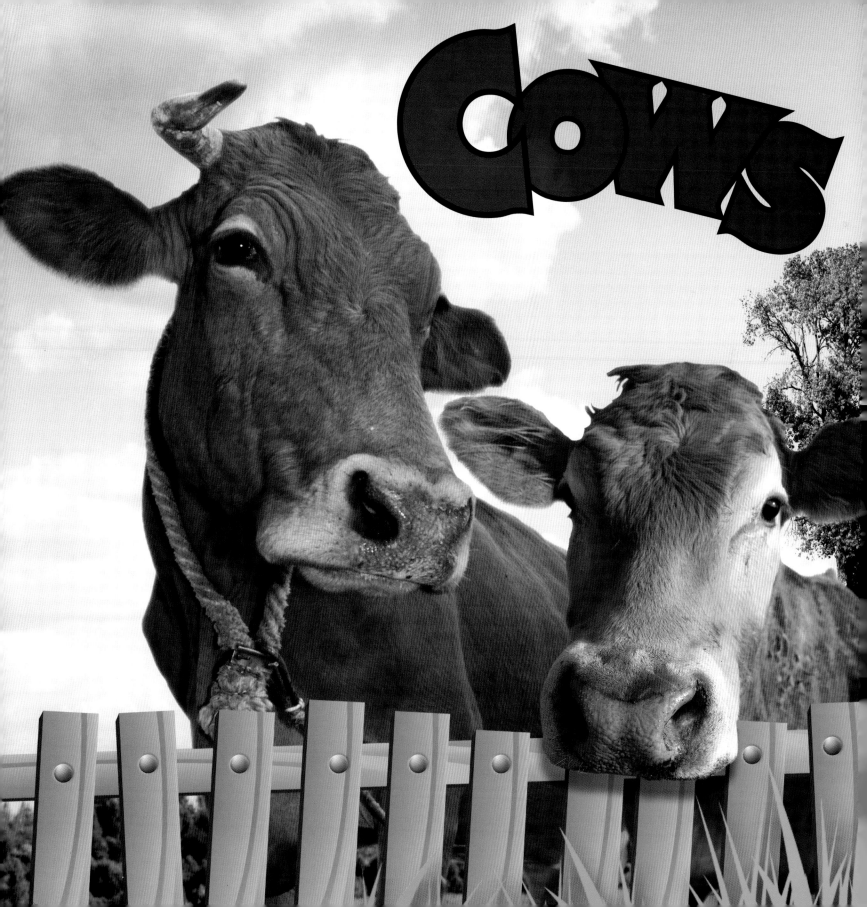

Cows

What are Cows?

Cows are large farm animals. They have hoofs on their feet with two toes.

Cows are mammals, which means they are covered in fur and feed their babies with milk. Milk is made in a special place on a cow's body, called an udder.

head

hoof

⇧ A hoof has two toes.

Cows and bulls are large animals with hoofs and horns. ⇨

Cows have long tails with hair at the end. They flick their tails around to keep flies away. Some cows have horns on their head. Bulls, or male cows, have the biggest horns.

horn

tail

udder

⬆ Cows and bulls can use their horns to attack other animals, or to fight each other.

Farmyard Fact!

Hoofs are hard and they protect an animal's feet. They are similar to your nails, which protect your fingertips and toes.

Cows on the Farm

Farmers keep cows for their milk and their meat. Cows live in groups called herds.

Thousands of years ago, cows were wild animals, but now they live on farms. Most cows are about 60 inches (1.5 meters) tall. That's the height of a small car.

⇐ Adult cows are large, strong animals.

Male cows are called bulls. Female cows are called cows. Young cows are called calves.

Cows are old enough to ⇨ have calves when they are about two years old.

⇩ Cows and bulls spend most of their day lying on the grass.

calf

cow

Farmyard Fact!
Cows have very good eyesight. They can see in front, to the side and even behind!

13

Where do Cows Live?

Cows that are kept for their milk are called dairy cows. They live on dairy farms.

Dairy cows spend most of their time in barns or in fields. If the cows spend the day in fields, they have shelters to keep out of the sun, rain, and wind. At night, they sleep in barns.

⇧ Shelters are safe, dry places where cows can rest.

Cows that live in barns are kept in **pens**. The floor is covered in sand or straw to keep the cows warm.

⇐ Farmers clean the pens every day.

⇓ The fields where cows live are called **pastures**.

pen

barn

Farmyard Fact!
Cows sleep lying down. They only need to sleep for about four hours a night, but they sometimes nap during the day.

What do Cows Eat?

Cows are herbivores, which means they only eat plants. Farmers make sure their cows have plenty of food.

Most cows can **graze** on grass in the field, or they are fed **hay**.

On some farms, cows are also fed with grains, such as corn and barley. They may be given **vitamins**, too.

⬅ A cow can spend seven hours a day grazing on grass.

Farmers put water **troughs** in the fields and barns. Then the cows can drink whenever they want to.

⇧ Cows eat from a food trough that is called a manger.

⇧ Every day, the farmer puts fresh water in the drinking trough.

Farmyard Fact!

Cows don't chew the grass very much before they swallow it. Later, the grass comes back into their mouth so they can chew it again! This is called "chewing the cud."

The Daily Life of a Cow

Cows are also known as cattle. They spend most of their time feeding or resting.

Beef cattle spend the day grazing in fields. Dairy cattle often live in **cowsheds** because they have to be milked every day.

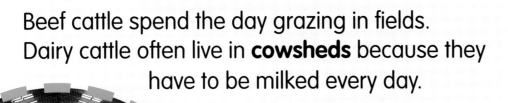

⇐ Dairy cows are kept in pens, ready for milking time.

Long-haired cattle ⇨ are kept outdoors to stay cool.

Farmers check their cattle to make sure they are healthy. They trim their cattle's hoofs to stop them getting too long and cracking.

⬇ Hoof trimming does not hurt cows. It help to keep their feet in good shape.

Farmyard Fact!
A dairy cow can drink more than 25 gallons (100 liters) of water every day. That's as much as a bathtub of water!

19

The Life Cycle of a Cow

Baby cows, or calves, grow inside their mothers. This time is called a pregnancy.

Calves are born in spring. The farmer helps a cow when it is time for her to give birth. Sometimes vets are also needed.

2

1

⬆ When a calf is born, the mother licks it clean, and soon it can stand up.

⬅ Cows are pregnant for about nine months.

3

↓ The calves move to barns or fields, and the life cycle begins again.

4

⬆ The calf drinks its mother's milk to grow strong and healthy.

Farmyard fact!
Most cows give birth to just one calf at a time, but sometimes a cow has **twins**.

21

Beef Cattle

Beef cattle are kept for their meat. They often live on big farms called ranches.

Farmers round up their beef cattle when it is time for them to go to **market**. The cattle will then be sold for food.

⇦ Ranch farmers often ride horses, and are called **cowboys** or cowgirls.

The meat from cattle will be sold for food. The skin of cattle is used to make leather.

The meat we get from ➡ cattle is called beef.

⬇ A farmer checks his herd is all healthy.

Farmyard Fact!
Shoes, bags, clothes, belts, and even furniture are often made of cow leather.

Dairy Cattle

Farmers have to milk dairy cows at least once a day. A cow can make up to 5 gallons (20 liters) of milk each day.

The milk from dairy cattle is then **pasteurized** and sold in stores, or used to make other dairy products, such as cheese.

⇧ Milking machines take the milk from a cow's udder quickly and easily.

⇩ At the dairy, milk is pasteurized and put into bottles or cartons.

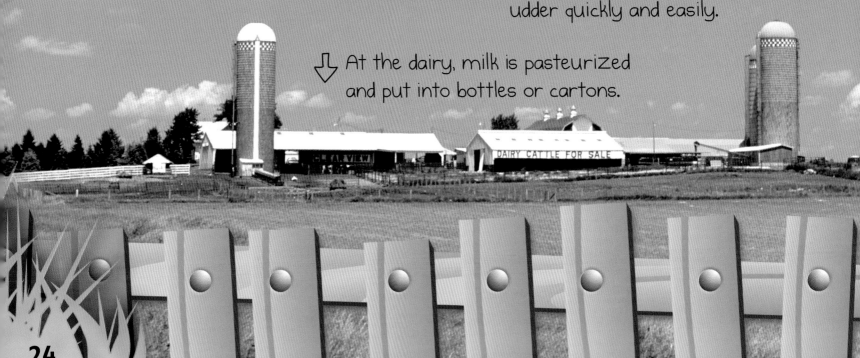

CLEAR VIEW

DAIRY CATTLE FOR SALE

⇩ The milk is cooled down and put in a tanker.

3

2

⇧ It is then sold in stores and supermarkets. The milk can also be made into dairy products such as cheese.

Farmyard Fact!
When milk is pasteurized, it is heated to kill bacteria, or bugs, that might be living in it. It is then safe to drink.

Breeds of Cattle

There are hundreds of different types of cattle. Each type is called a breed.

Some breeds are best for their milk, while others are best for their meat.

Many dairy farmers keep Holstein cows. Their fur is black and white, but no two cows have exactly the same pattern.

← Holstein cows produce milk for about six years.

Holstein cow

Farmyard Fact!

Many foods contain milk. Ask an adult to help you look in your fridge to find some of them.

Ankole cattle live in Africa. They are kept for their milk, not for their meat.

Ankole cattle grow very long, curved horns. ⇨

Herefords are large beef cattle. Farmers all over the world like to keep Herefords because they are very good for meat.

⇩ Hereford cattle have brown bodies and white faces.

Ankole bull

Hereford cow

27

Pigs

What are Pigs?

Pigs are mammals. All mammals have a hairy body and feed their babies with milk.

Pigs have small eyes but their noses are large. They have a very good sense of smell.

tail

Pigs have a barrel-shaped body, thin legs, and a big head.

trotter

⇧ A pig's trotter is cloven. This means it has two parts.

Pigs have hoofed feet and walk on two toes, like sheep and cows. Their feet are called trotters.

tusk

head

shoulder

snout

⬆ Wild pigs have more hair than farm pigs. They are smaller, faster and often have **tusks**.

Farmyard fact!
A male pig is called a boar. Female pigs are called sows. Baby pigs are called piglets.

Pigs on the Farm

Pigs are also known as hogs or swine. They are kept on farms for their meat.

They live in family groups, called herds. In the wild, they live in woods where they **forage**, or look for, for food.

⇩ Farm pigs like to spend time outdoors.

Pigs can weigh up to 1,000 pounds (450 kilograms) and are about 28 inches (70 centimeters) tall—that's almost as tall as a child!

Pigs are very clean animals. ⇩
Sows are friendly, too.

Farmyard fact!

Pigs do not like hot weather because they cannot sweat. Sweating helps an animal to cool down.

Where do Pigs Live?

Most pigs live in large pig pens or in fields on farms. There can be several pens in one barn.

Sows are often kept in pens together. Sometimes, sows are kept alone in small pens called stalls.

Boars are kept in separate pens because they often fight with each other. Their pens have high fences so they cannot jump over them.

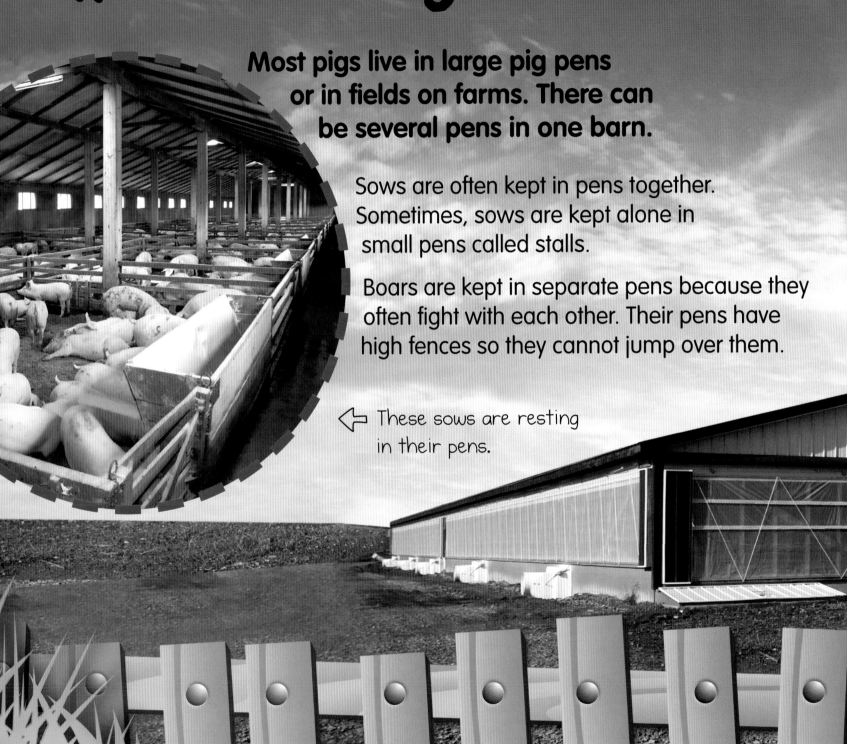

← These sows are resting in their pens.

Some farmers give their
pigs straw to sleep on.

Large indoor pig farms
are called **piggeries.**
Pig food is stored in
big metal tanks.

Farmyard Fact!
Pigs used to live on small
farms, but now many of
them live in piggeries.
Thousands of pigs live
in just one piggery.

35

What do Pigs Eat?

Pigs can eat many things, such as meat, fruit, and grass. Animals that eat different foods are called omnivores.

Pigs get their water from **drinkers**. A sow can drink more than 8 gallons (30 liters) of water every day.

⇐ This young pig is sucking water from a drinker.

Pigs eat food from troughs. Most pigs eat pellets that contain vitamins to keep them healthy.

⬇ Pigs like to walk in fields where they can find fresh grass to eat.

⬇ Pellets are made from **cereals** and vitamins.

Farmyard Fact!

A pig has 44 teeth. Wild pigs grow large teeth, called tusks. Boars use their tusks to fight each other.

Living Outside

Some pigs live in outdoor shelters in fields. Their shelters are called sties, huts, or arcs.

The shelters protect the pigs from hot, cold, and wet weather. The pigs eat food, such as grass and roots, in the field.

⇐ This type of metal shelter is called an arc.

Farmyard Fact!

Truffles are a type of rare mushroom that grows underground. Some farmers train pigs to find the truffles using their sense of smell.

Pigs like to lie in mud. It keeps their skin cool, and stops them from getting sunburned.

⇧ **Free-range** piglets can stay with their mother.

⇩ Pigs that live outside are called outdoor-reared, or free-range, pigs.

The Life Cycle of a Pig

Sows are pregnant for about four months before they give birth. Baby pigs are called piglets.

Sows can give birth to a litter of about 10 piglets at a time. The piglets become adults at about two years old.

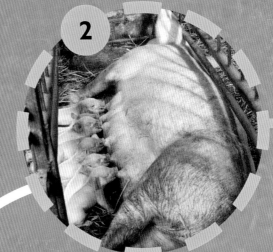

⇧ When piglets are born, they drink their mother's milk. It helps them to grow and stay healthy.

⇦ The farmer puts the sow into a **farrowing** stall about one week before she is due to give birth.

3 ⬅ The piglets live in a nursery pen for five to 10 weeks.

⬇ When they are about 10 weeks old, the piglets can go to the sheds or fields. Then the life cycle begins again.

4

Farmyard fact!
Piglets move into a separate area when their mother wants to sleep. Otherwise, she might crush them!

Life on the Farm

Pigs spend most of the day eating, drinking, and resting.

Farmers clean the pens regularly, removing all the dirty straw and putting new straw down. The pigs like to sniff around in the straw.

Inspectors check that the pigs are kept in clean, safe pens, and that they are healthy. When they are old enough, the pigs are taken from the farm, and sold for meat.

Farm pigs can eat or drink ⇨ whenever they want to.

⇦ Young pigs like to be together. Most pens hold pigs that are all the same age.

Farmyard Fact!

Pigs are so clever they can learn how to open farm gates. Some people like pigs so much they keep them as pets!

Why do We Farm Pigs?

Most pigs are kept on farms for their meat. The meat that comes from pigs is called pork.

Pork is packaged and sold to supermarkets or shops. Pork can also be used to make foods such as sausages and bacon.

⬇ Pigs live on the farm until it is time for them to be sold for meat.

Some pork is used to make ham and bacon. The meat is stored in dry salt or salty water, before other flavors are added to it. This type of pork is called **cured meat**.

⇧ Ham is a type of cured meat.

Farmyard fact!
People have been eating sausages for thousands of years. Most sausages are made from pork and cereals.

Breeds of Pig

There are many different types of pig. Each type is called a breed.

Large white pigs are one of the world's most popular breeds. Farmers are able to keep them outdoors, or in pig sheds.

⇦ Large white sows are very good mothers.

large white pig

Farmyard Fact!

Mangalitza pigs are covered in a layer of curly fur. It helps them to stay warm during long, cold winters.

Kune kune pigs are rare. Their hair can be straight or curly, and it is often spotted. They have short legs and a small snout.

The name of a Kune kune pig means "fat and round."

Mangalitza pigs are kept on farms in Europe. Their meat is used for ham, sausage, and bacon.

Mangalitza pigs are also known as woolly pigs.

Kune kune pig

Mangalitza pig

Sheep

What are Sheep?

Sheep are mammals. All mammals have fur and drink their mother's milk when they are born.

A sheep's feet are called hoofs. Each hoof is divided into two large toes. Most sheep have long white, cream, brown, or black fur.

⇐ Sheep have thick fur called wool. It helps them to stay warm in the winter.

hoof

toe

Sheep have a large body and four thin legs. ⇒

Rams, or male sheep, often have large, curly horns. They use their horns for fighting other rams.

← Horns are made of bone and have sharp tips.

Farmyard fact!

Sheep are noisy animals. The noise a sheep makes is called a bleat. It sounds like "baa-baa."

51

Sheep on the Farm

Farmers all over the world keep sheep for their wool, meat, or milk. A sheep's wool is used to make clothing.

Most sheep are about 20 inches (0.5 meters) tall. That's about the height from the floor to your shoulder.

← Female sheep and lambs are friendly animals.

⬇ Female sheep and lambs live together in flocks.

Farmyard Fact!

Sheep have lived on farms for thousands of years. They were probably one of the first animals that humans kept for food.

Sheep live in groups, called flocks.
A female sheep is called a ewe.
A male sheep is called a ram.
Young sheep are called lambs.

Ewes are smaller than rams. ⇨
Some ewes have horns.

ewe

lamb

flock

Where do Sheep Live?

Most sheep live in pastures, or fields.
Some sheep live on hills or mountains.

Sheep are tough animals that can live in all sorts of weather, from snow and rain to hot, dry conditions.

⇐ Their thick woollen coats help sheep to keep warm in snowy weather.

Sheep may be put in an area with a fence around it, called a pen. They can also be kept indoors. Farmers have to keep indoor pens clean, warm, and dry.

Indoor pens protect sheep from ⇨ dogs and foxes that hunt them.

⇩ At the end of the day, the farmer puts his sheep in a pen.

Farmyard Fact!

Lambs have their own special areas in a pen, where ewes cannot go. The lambs stay here when they want to escape from their moms!

55

What do Sheep Eat?

Sheep graze, or chew, on grass. They eat a lot of food in a short time, and then they rest for a while.

During the summer, sheep can feed on fresh grass, but in winter the farmer gives them hay. Hay is dried grass.

⬇ Farmers clean the troughs every day, and fill them with fresh water.

⬆ Sheep have sharp teeth that can cut hay and grass.

Farmers also give the sheep food pellets, which are made of grains such as corn and oats. These food pellets contain lots of vitamins.

⇧ Pellets help sheep to grow big and strong.

Sheep need to drink a lot of water to stay healthy. They drink water out of troughs.

Troughs are normally long, ⇨ shallow and made of metal.

trough

Farmyard fact!

Sheep spend around seven hours a day eating. Their favorite times to graze are early morning and late afternoon.

The Life Cycle of Sheep

Most lambs are born in spring, when the weather is getting warmer and the grass has started to grow.

A ewe gives birth to ⇩ one or two lambs at a time.

⇧ After the lamb is born, its mother licks it clean.

Farmyard Fact!

A lamb can find its mother in a flock by listening for her bleat. Every sheep's bleat sounds different.

3 ⇐ Soon, it can stand up by itself and feed from its mother's milk.

⇓ After a few days, the lambs can live in pens or outdoors. Then the life cycle begins again.

4

The Daily Life of Sheep

Sheep spend most of their day walking, eating, and resting.

Ewes and lambs stay together in a flock, but rams are kept away to stop them from fighting.

Farmers train **sheepdogs** to make the flock move towards the pasture, or into pens and shelters.

⇩ Sheepdogs are trained to stay behind a flock. They need to be both clever and gentle.

Vets visit the sheep and give them medicine when they are sick. They also give sheep a special bath, called a sheep-dip, to keep their skin healthy.

Farmers give their sheep medicines. ⇨
This stops them from getting sick.

Farmyard fact!

In some countries, sheep are kept on hills or mountains. **Shepherds** travel on horseback or on motorbikes to check that their flocks are safe.

Why do We Farm Sheep?

Most sheep are kept by farmers for their wool or their meat.

A farmer may choose some lambs that will grow to become ewes or rams. The others will be used for meat. Their meat is known as lamb.

Farmyard Fact!

Sheep are often kept for their milk. Sheep's milk is mostly used to make cheese.

Sheep that are more than two years old are also used for meat. Their meat is called mutton.

These chops have ⇨ come from lambs.

⇦ Farmers move their sheep on to a truck, so they can be taken to market.

Sheep Shearing

At least once a year, sheep that are kept for their wool need to have a haircut.

Cutting the wool from a sheep is called shearing. Having no fur helps the sheep stay cool in summer. Farmers use **shears**, or scissors, to cut the wool.

⇧ A farmer uses shears to remove the wool, without hurting the ewe.

Farmyard Fact!
A fleece is washed and combed before it is turned into woollen yarn. Special colorings, called dyes, are added to yarn.

If the wool is removed in one piece, it is called a fleece. Most wool is used to make clothes and carpets.

Wool can be used to knit ⇨ clothes and blankets.

⇩ After shearing, sheep look thin. Their wool starts to grow back straight away.

Breeds of Sheep

Merino sheep

There are many different breeds, or kinds, of sheep. Most sheep are kept for either their meat or their wool.

Farmers keep merino sheep for their fine, soft wool. It is used to make clothes.

⇧ Merino ewes have white faces. They do not grow horns.

Farmyard Fact!

Little Portland lambs are born with orange-red wool. It changes color to white or gray when they are a few months old.

Jacob sheep have black-and-white fleeces, and long horns. They are mostly kept by farmers for their meat.

Blackface sheep are mostly kept for their meat. They are very strong and can live on cold, rainy mountains.

⇩ Jacob sheep do not grow very thick winter coats.

Jacob sheep

⇩ The wool from blackface sheep is strong. It can be used to make carpets.

Blackface sheep

Chickens

What are Chickens?

Chickens are birds. Like all birds, chickens have feathers and beaks, and they lay eggs.

Chickens have wings, but they are not very good at flying. Farmers clip some of their wing feathers, to stop chickens flying away from the farm.

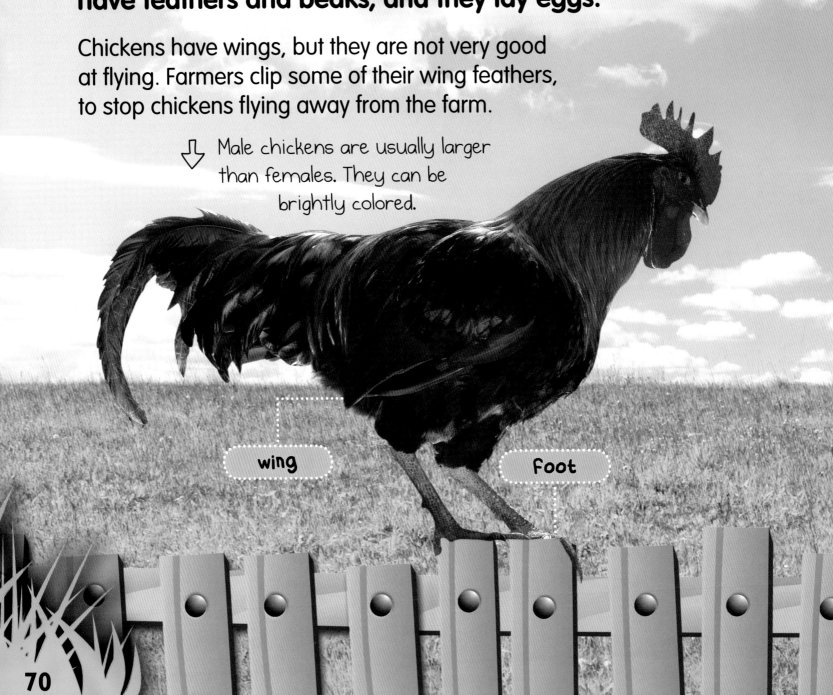

⇩ Male chickens are usually larger than females. They can be brightly colored.

wing

foot

A chicken's mouth is called a beak.

There is a piece of flesh on top of a chicken's head that looks like a crown. It is called a comb.

comb

beak

head

wattle

⬆ Another piece of flesh hangs below the chicken's beak. This is called a wattle.

Farmyard Fact!

Combs and wattles help chickens keep cool. The male chicken's bright-red wattle helps him to attract females.

71

Chickens on the Farm

Chickens are kept on farms all over the world. There are hundreds of different breeds, or types, of chicken.

Chickens are large birds. They measure about 12 to 16 inches (30 to 40 centimeters) from their feet to the top of their head. That's about as tall as a box of cereal.

NEW!
FRUITY CEREAL
625g

⇦ Chickens can fluff out their feathers, which makes them look even bigger.

Chickens lived in the wild until people began keeping chickens for food. Now, there are more chickens in the world than people. Most chickens are kept for their meat or eggs.

← Hens can be very friendly, and like to be stroked.

↑ The large chicken is a cockerel. The other chickens are hens.

Farmyard fact!

Male chickens are called roosters or cockerels, and females are called hens. Baby chickens are called chicks.

Where do Chickens Live?

Most chickens live on poultry farms. A poultry farmer keeps only birds such as chickens and turkeys.

Chickens spend the night in barns. The floors of barns are covered in straw, and there are **perches** for the chickens to sleep on.

During the day, the chickens wander around the farmyard in the fresh air.

⇩ When the sun is shining, the hens go outside. If it rains, they can go back into their barn.

⇩ Hens grip onto their perches with their strong, clawed feet.

Farmyard Fact!
Chickens often sleep with one eye open, or they tuck their head under one of their wings.

What do Chickens Eat?

Chickens do not have any teeth, so they have to eat small pieces of food. They swallow this food whole.

Farmers put out water and **feeders** for their chickens. Feeders are full of chicken feed, which is made of grains such as wheat and barley.

⬆ Chickens spend a lot of time eating. They peck at their food.

Farmyard Fact!
Farmers give hens bits of broken seashells, called grit, to eat. Grit helps hens lay eggs with strong shells.

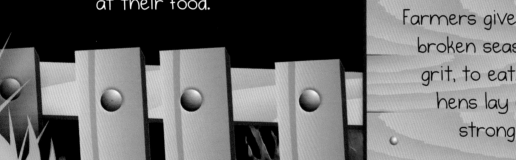

← Grains of wheat are small and full of goodness.

When chickens go outside, they scratch the ground with their claws. They look for worms, insects, and small seeds to eat.

Sometimes, chickens ⇨ eat grass.

The Life Cycle of Chickens

Hens start to lay eggs when they are about five months old. They can lay up to 300 eggs in one year.

Eggs will not grow into chicks unless a rooster has **mated** with the hen, and **fertilized** her eggs.

Hens lay their eggs ⇨ in nests. They sit on the eggs to keep them warm.

1

2

⇧ About three weeks later, the chicks are ready to hatch out.

3

⇧ Once the chicks' feathers have dried, they become fluffy.

4

The chicks grow into adults in a few months, and the life cycle begins again. ⇨

Farmyard fact!

The **yolk** inside an egg would have been food for a chick, if the egg had been fertilized.

Why do We Farm Chickens?

Poultry farmers collect the fertilized eggs. They keep them in a place called a hatchery.

Hatcheries are warm places where eggs can hatch into chicks. A few days after they have **hatched**, the chicks are sorted into two groups.

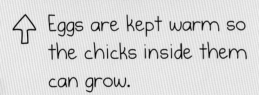

⬆ Eggs are kept warm so the chicks inside them can grow.

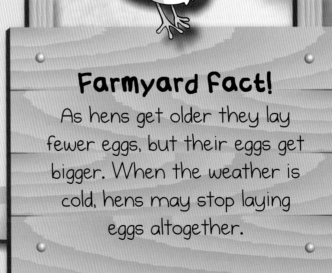

Farmyard Fact!

As hens get older they lay fewer eggs, but their eggs get bigger. When the weather is cold, hens may stop laying eggs altogether.

Some chicks will become **layers**. These chickens will lay eggs to be eaten, or eggs that will become chicks. Some chicks will become broiler chickens. **Broilers** are birds that are grown for their meat.

⬆ Chicks peck at food in the red feeders.

⬅ This chick is still hatching from its egg.

Daily Life on the Farm

Chickens live in groups called flocks. Every few weeks, farm inspectors check that the chickens are being kept well and are healthy.

Some poultry farmers let their chickens roam outside. They are called free-range chickens, and they lay free-range eggs.

⬇ Little chicks stay near the hens, where they feel safe.

Free-range chickens are able to walk around and look for food. At night, they return to their barns, or to small houses called coops, to sleep.

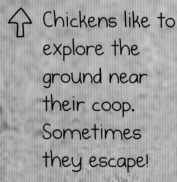

⇧ Chickens like to explore the ground near their coop. Sometimes they escape!

Farmyard Fact!
Chickens love dust and dirt. They ruffle their feathers in the dirt to help keep their feathers clean and in good condition.

From the Farm to the Table

Farmers keep hens so they can sell their eggs. Some farmers sell their chickens as food.

Eggs are put into egg boxes. The eggs are sent to stores and supermarkets. Eggs can also be used to make other foods, such as cakes and cookies.

These hens are layers. They will each lay about five eggs a week.

Egg boxes hold eggs ⬆ in place, so they do not move around and break.

Farmyard Fact!

When eggs are cooked, the heat changes the runny insides of the egg into a solid.

When broiler chickens are more than 20 weeks old, they are taken to a slaughterhouse. Their meat is packed and sold fresh or frozen in stores and supermarkets.

Chicken meat is full of goodness ⇨ to help you stay healthy.

Breeds of Chicken

Chickens come in all shapes, sizes, and colors. The different kinds of chicken are called breeds.

Leghorns have white feathers and are mostly kept on farms for their eggs. Most breeds of chicken lay white, cream, or brown eggs, but some lay blue or dark-brown eggs.

⇧ Farmers get paid more for large eggs, or for ones with different colors.

leghorn chicken

⇧ Leghorn hens are fast movers, and can fly over fences.

Farmyard Fact!

Buff Orpington chickens are very popular. They are a light-gold color and lay large brown eggs.

Polish crested chicken

Some breeds are kept for their looks. Chickens with crests, strong colors, and pretty feathers are popular.

Bantams are small chickens. They are often very colorful and can be kept as pets.

⇧ Polish crested chickens have fluffy feathers on their head, called a crest.

bantam chicken

⇧ Bantam hens lay very small eggs.

Horses and Ponies

What are Horses and Ponies?

Horses and ponies are large animals. They have four long legs with hoofs. Each hoof is made of a hard, bony material.

Horses grow long, straight hair on their head and neck. This hair is called a mane. It is the same color as the horse's tail.

Horses and ponies can be different colors, such as brown or gray. Their fur may have **markings**, too.

tail

hoof

Horses and ponies are covered in fur. It helps them stay warm.

head

mane

A blaze is a wide marking on the face.

A star is a white marking between the eyes.

A stripe is a thin marking on the face.

Farmyard fact!
Very few horses and ponies have totally black fur. Most black horses have some white markings.

Horses and Ponies on the Farm

In the past, farmers used horses and ponies to pull heavy carts and plows.

Today, most farmers use machines, so horses and ponies are kept on farms for riding.

Farmers can measure how tall a horse is by using their hands. They measure from the ground to the withers, or shoulders.

⬆ One "hand" is the width of an adult's hand (4 inches (10 centimeters)). This horse is 15 hands high.

Horses are more than 60 inches (150 centimeters), or 15 hands tall. Ponies are less than 58 inches (147 centimeters), or 14.5 hands, tall.

horse

pony

Farmyard Fact!
The smallest kind of pony is a Shetland pony. Many Shetlands are no more than 40 inches (1 meter), or 10 hands, tall.

Where do Horses and Ponies Live?

During the daytime, horses and ponies are kept in fields. They spend their time exercising and eat grass.

Farmers normally build shelters in the fields. The horses go to the shelters when they are too hot, too cold, or too wet.

⇐ A shelter protects the animals from the sun, rain, and wind.

Horses and ponies ⇒ need plenty of space to exercise.

At the end of the day, farmers bring horses and ponies back from the fields and into stables for the night.

← The stables are warm and dry.

Farmyard fact!

Stables need to be cleaned out every day. This is known as **mucking out.**

95

What do Horses and Ponies Eat?

Horses and ponies mostly eat grass and hay. Farmers also give them water and some dry food.

Horses should not eat too much food at a time because it can make them ill. Sometimes, farmers give their horses and ponies a healthy treat. They love to eat apples and carrots.

Horses and ponies graze on grass. ⇨

Dry food is called hard feed. Bran, oats, pony nuts, and maize are types of hard feed.

⇧ Hard feed contains vitamins to keep horses healthy.

Hay is dried grass. ⇨ Horses also eat hay.

Farmyard Fact!

An average horse eats about 22 pounds (10 kilograms) of food a day. That's the weight of 10 bags of sugar!

Looking After Horses and Ponies

Farmers ride their horses every day, or let them into a field. Horses like to walk around and graze on grass.

Horses need to be kept clean. Farmers groom, or brush, their horses and ponies to keep them healthy.

A **blacksmith** looks after the horses' hoofs. They fit horses with shoes to stop their hoofs cracking from walking on hard ground.

⇧ First, the blacksmith takes off the old horseshoe.

⇦ The hoof is clipped and a new shoe is put on.

Tails and manes are brushed ⇨ to remove dirt, mud, and hay.

⇩ In the wild, horses live in groups called herds.

Farmyard Fact!

Blackmiths change horses' shoes about eight times every year. That's about once every six weeks.

Riding Horses and Ponies

Most horses and ponies on farms are used for riding. Children usually ride ponies because ponies are smaller than horses.

Farmers also enter their horses and ponies into shows. They take part in competitions such as show jumping.

⬆ Most horses and ponies like to jump fences.

Farmyard Fact!

Horses and ponies are around five years old when they start taking part in competitions.

The **tack** room is where farmers keep the saddles and **bridles** that they use to ride horses and ponies. ⇨

Riders sit on saddles and use reins ⇩ to control the horse or pony.

bridle

saddle

The Life Cycle of a Horse

Male horses and ponies are called stallions. Females are called mares.

Baby horses and ponies are called foals. A mare is pregnant for about 11 months before giving birth to her foal.

⇧ A foal drinks its mother's milk for about six months.

⇦ A mare licks her foal clean after it is born.

3

A foal becomes an adult when it is about three years old. Then the life cycle begins again.

Farmyard Fact!

Just like humans, foals are born with no teeth. Their teeth begin to grow when foals are one week old.

Horse and Pony Breeds

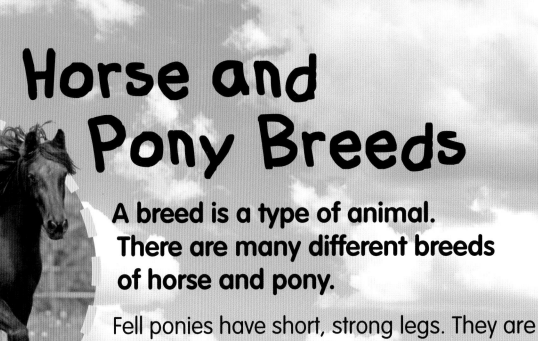

A breed is a type of animal. There are many different breeds of horse and pony.

Fell ponies have short, strong legs. They are used for farm work, such as herding sheep. They can also carry heavy loads, or pull carts.

Fell pony

⇧ Most breeds of pony are very strong.

Farmyard Fact!

There are more than 200 different breeds of horse in the world.

Appaloosa horses are used for riding and jumping. They have white, brown, or black markings.

The markings on this Appaloosa are called "blanket with spots." ⇨

Quarter horses are common in the USA, where they work on cattle ranches. Quarter horses are very strong and fast.

Cowboys often ride ⇨ quarter horses.

Appaloosa horse

Quarter horse

Hard-working Horses

The largest horses are called draft horses. They are hard-working and strong.

Some farmers need draft horses to pull carts and plow fields, but most farmers use machines, such as tractors, to do their heavy work.

Draft horses have hair around their hoofs. This hair is called "feather."

harness

feather

Draft horses are sometimes entered into competitions and horse shows. Their tack is covered with decorations made of brass. Their manes and tails are brushed and braided for horse shows.

⇧ Draft horses have a large head and strong neck.

Farmyard Fact!

Drauft horses can be more than 72 inches (180 centimeters), or 18 hands, tall. That's as tall as an adult man!

Glossary

Blacksmith
Blacksmiths are people who look after horses' hoofs and fit their shoes.

Bridle
This is used to control a horse. A bridle is made of leather straps and the reins are attached to it.

Broiler
A broiler chicken is one that is kept for its meat.

Cattle
Cattle are animals with hoofs. Cows, bulls, and calves are cattle.

Cereal
This is a type of food that comes from grains, such as wheat, oats, and corn.

Cowboy
A person who rides horses on a cattle ranch is called a cowboy or cowgirl.

Cowshed
This is a large farm building where cows live or are milked.

Cured meat
This meat has been changed by adding salt to it.

Drinker
Animals can get fresh water from drinkers.

Farrowing
This is the time when a sow gives birth to her piglets.

Feeder
Food containers for chickens are called feeders.

Fertilize
When a special cell from a male joins a female's egg to form a new living thing.

Forage
When animals forage they are searching for food.

Free-range
Animals that are able to live outdoors, and have plenty of space, are called free-range.

Graze
Animals that feed on growing grass are said to be grazing.

Hatching
This is when a chick
breaks out of its egg.

Hay
Grass that has been cut
and dried so it can be
given to animals to eat.

Inspector
A person who checks
that animals on farms
are looked after well is
called an inspector.

Layer
A hen that is kept
for her eggs is called
a layer.

Market
This is a place
where farmers gather
to sell their animals.

Markings
Some horses and ponies
have patches of color
on their fur. These are
called markings.

Mate
When animals come together
to fertilize the female's eggs
they are said to mate.

Mucking out
When someone cleans a
stable they are mucking out.

Pasteurized
This means heating milk to make it safe to drink.

Pasture
This is a field of grass where animals, such as cows and sheep, can graze.

Pen
A pen is a small area that is surrounded with a fence. Animals are kept in pens

Perch
The place where hens like to stand or sit is called a perch.

Piggery
This is a large indoor pig farm.

Plow
Farmers have to plow, or turn the soil over, before they can plant their seeds. They use a plow to do this job.

Poultry
Birds that are kept on farms are called poultry. The word "poultry" is also used for the meat that comes from those birds.

Ranch
A ranch is a very large farm.

Shears
Shears are tools used for cutting the fur, or wool, from a sheep's body.

Sheepdog
Sheepdogs are dogs that have been trained to move flocks of sheep.

Shepherd
A shepherd is a person who looks after sheep.

Tack
Stirrups, reins, bridles, and saddles are all called tack.

Trough
A trough is a long, narrow container that is used for giving an animal food or water.

Tusk
This is a long, pointed tooth.

Twins
When an animal gives birth to two young at the same time, they are called twins.

Vitamins
These are found in food. They help animals, and people, to grow well and stay healthy.

Yolk
The yellow part of an egg is called the yolk.

Index

Notes for Parents and Teachers

- Look through the book together, talk about the pictures and find new words in the glossary.

- Talk about the basic needs that animals and humans share, such as food, space, and shelter. Encourage the child to think about how wild animals get their food and find shelter.

- It is fun to find ways that animals are similar, or different, to one another—and observing these things is a core science skill. Children could draw pictures of animals with four legs, or ones that eat plants, for example, and go on to identify those that are both plant-eaters and four-legged.

- Be prepared for questions about how animals become the meat that we eat. It helps children understand this part of the food chain if they can see it in context: all animals live and die, and farm animals are bred for this purpose.

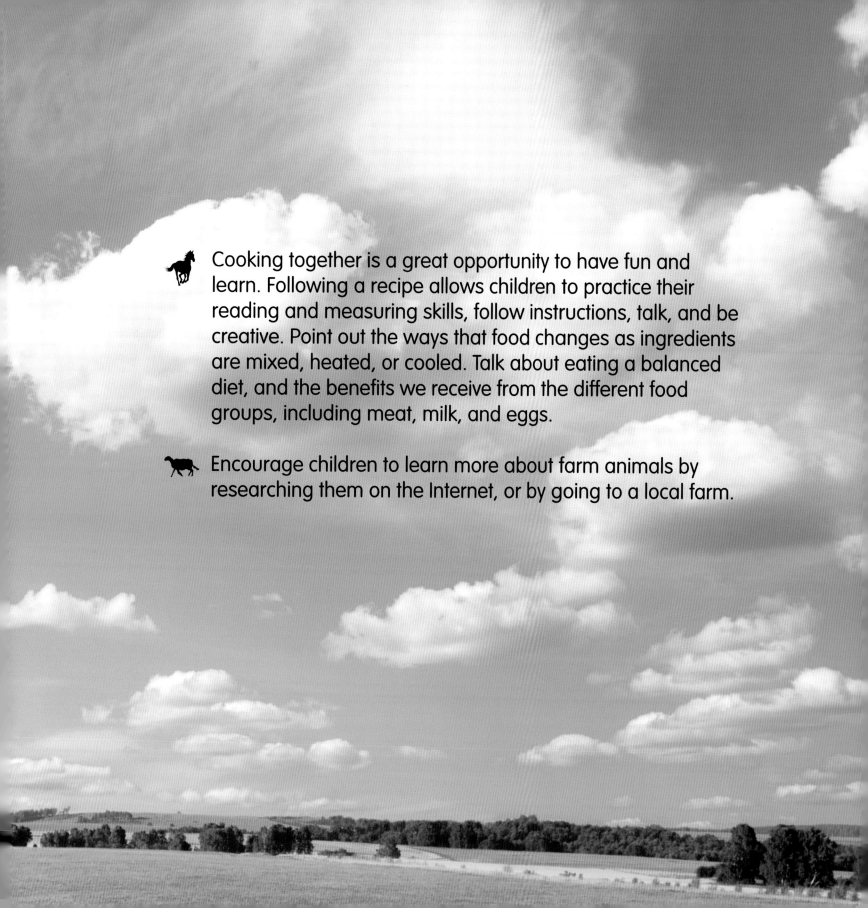

Cooking together is a great opportunity to have fun and learn. Following a recipe allows children to practice their reading and measuring skills, follow instructions, talk, and be creative. Point out the ways that food changes as ingredients are mixed, heated, or cooled. Talk about eating a balanced diet, and the benefits we receive from the different food groups, including meat, milk, and eggs.

Encourage children to learn more about farm animals by researching them on the Internet, or by going to a local farm.